PATRICK DESJARLAIT

Conversations with a Native American Artist

as recorded by
Neva Williams

Runestone Press • Minneapolis

RUNESTONE PRESS • ᚱᚢᚾᛏᛋᛏᛉᚾ

rune (ro͞on) *n* **1 a :** one of the earliest written alphabets used in northern Europe, dating back to A.D. 200; **b :** an alphabet character believed to have magic powers; **c :** a charm; **d :** an Old Norse or Finnish poem. **2 :** a poem or incantation of mysterious significance, often carved in stone.

Patrick DesJarlait: Conversations with a Native American Artist is a fully revised and updated edition of *Patrick DesJarlait: the Story of an American Indian Artist*, a title previously published by Lerner Publications Company. The text is completely reset in 13/15 Clearface, and new photographs and captions have been added.

The publisher has made every effort to contact and credit the current owners of all artworks in this edition. If any errors have been made, please contact the publisher.

Words in **bold** type are listed in a glossary that begins on page 54.

Library of Congress Cataloging-in-Publication Data
   Patrick DesJarlait: conversations with a Native American artist /
as recorded by Neva Williams.
     p.   cm.
   ISBN 0-8225-3151-8 (lib. bdg.)
   1. DesJarlait, Patrick, 1921–1972—Juvenile literature. 2.
Ojibwa Indians—Biography—Juvenile literature. 3. Ojibwa artists—
Biography—Juvenile literature. I. Williams, Neva. II. Title.
E99.C6D477 1995
977.6'82—dc20   94-6535
                                                        [B]
                                                        CIP

Manufactured in the United States of America

1 2 3 4 5 6 – I/JR – 00 99 98 97 96 95

CONTENTS

A NOTE FROM THE PUBLISHER

I first met Patrick DesJarlait in 1972. At that time, Neva Williams outlined her idea of interviewing the artist in a series of tape recordings. We discussed how those interviews and his artworks could be the basis for a book. Patrick DesJarlait was a kindly, likable person who showed great interest in the idea. Neva's taped interviews tell us about the life of this unique artist. He died later that same year.

DesJarlait's artwork lives on. Many of his paintings are displayed in museums and other public places. Several have won top awards in national art exhibitions.

DesJarlait often spoke to groups of students about his Native American heritage, using his art to illustrate the lifeways of his people. In this tradition, we hope that telling DesJarlait's story will help keep Native American arts and cultures alive.

Harry J. Lerner

INTRODUCTION

Patrick DesJarlait was an artist who belonged to the Red Lake Chippewa Band of northwestern Minnesota. He became known throughout the United States for his vivid paintings of **Chippewa** life and for his efforts to preserve Chippewa customs.

DesJarlait's people are also known as Ojibway and as Anishinabe. Since early times, the Chippewa have called themselves Anishinabe, which means "original people." Although Ojibway (also spelled Ojibwa or Ojibwe) is now the most frequently used term, Chippewa was more common when DesJarlait lived and worked.

DesJarlait was born at Red Lake Indian Reservation in 1921. His interest in art began in his early childhood. Even at the age of five, he loved to draw and sketch. As he grew older, DesJarlait developed and perfected the painting style that would become his trademark. He painted with watercolors, using bright, rich tones to intensify the subjects of his pictures. DesJarlait's paintings portrayed many traditions of the Red Lake Chippewa. Through his art, DesJarlait demonstrated his people's love and respect for their heritage and for the land on which they lived.

Patrick DesJarlait had a French grandfather from whom the artist inherited his French last name. French fur traders from Canada met the Chippewa of northwestern Minnesota in the 1700s. In the 1800s, U.S. citizens moved into the area, setting up **missions** to teach Christianity to the Native Americans. After Christianity was introduced to the Chippewa at Red Lake, parents commonly named their children after saints. DesJarlait was named for Saint Patrick.

Red Lake Indian Reservation

Held in common by members of the Red Lake Chippewa Band, Red Lake Indian Reservation covers an area the size of the state of Rhode Island. The **reservation** encompasses the Upper and Lower Red lakes, which together form the largest body of fresh water within any one state in the United States.

Red Lake Indian Reservation has rolling hills, thick forests, and many small lakes, ponds, bogs, and prairies. Winter temperatures in the region are very cold, often dropping to −25° F. The lakes freeze over, and snow blankets the land.

When the ice and snow melt each spring, wild blueberries, honeysuckle, and wintergreen sprout from the ground, and the buds

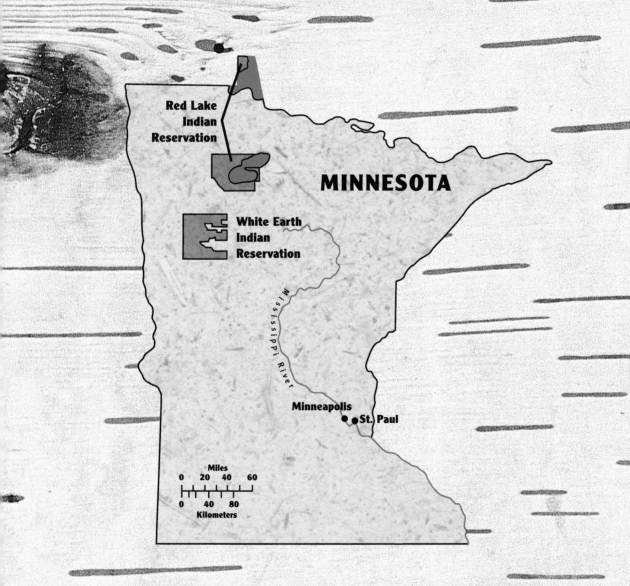

Red Lake
Indian
Reservation

MINNESOTA

White Earth
Indian
Reservation

Mississippi River

Minneapolis
St. Paul

Miles
0   20   40   60

0   40   80
Kilometers

Workers at Red Lake Indian Reservation process wild rice.

of new leaves appear on bare oak and maple trees. Most of the other trees at Red Lake are evergreens, such as pine, fir, and spruce. The woodlands are home to deer, moose, rabbits, wolves, bears, and many other wild animals. Pheasants and quail live in grassy areas, and ducks and geese flock to lakes and wetlands, which teem with fish.

To make their living, the people of Red Lake traditionally fished, hunted, farmed, cut lumber, and collected wild rice and maple syrup. In the 1920s, the reservation had four towns—Red Lake, Redby, Ponemah, and Little Rock—where many of the Red Lake Chippewa attended school and church. Although most of the residents of the reservation were Chippewa, some white people lived in these towns. The town of Red Lake also had a hospital that cared for mothers-to-be and new babies and that helped to fight diseases.

Life on the reservation was not easy. Many homes had no plumbing or central heating. Jobs were scarce at times. But the Red Lake Chippewa took pride in their culture and traditions, and most of them were determined to live at Red Lake as their ancestors had done.

1
MY CHILDHOOD AT RED LAKE

My earliest memories of Red Lake Reservation have a storybook quality. I remember beautiful tall trees, sparkling blue water, and pure white snow. There were acres of forested land on the reservation, and the clear lakes held almost every kind of local fish.

Nature had provided a perfect setting for a young boy growing up in northwestern Minnesota. I spent many hours of my childhood wandering through the woods, either by myself or with my friends. In the forests that surrounded my home, I found the animals and woodland scenes that became the subjects for my first drawings.

I remember spending happy days as a small child with my parents and my six brothers and sisters. I was the middle child. Two brothers and one sister were older than me, and two brothers and one sister were younger. My mother and father had their work cut out for them in providing all of us with food and security, but they seemed to enjoy our family life.

Untitled, 1972

Like many of the men at Red Lake, my father worked as a woodcutter for the Red Lake Timber Mill. The mill was in the town of Redby, a mile and a half away from our house. When I reached school age, my father became an independent lumberman and took contracts for cutting pulp wood and logs. He worked very long hours. On many winter nights he did not get home with his horse and sleigh until after dark.

The house that we lived in was built by my father. Most of my friends lived in small one- or two-room frame houses that were covered with tar paper. But our house was made of logs. It was warm and well built, with three bedrooms and one very large room that we used as both living room and kitchen. Since my older brothers and sister lived away at school most of the year, there was plenty of room in the house for our family.

Like most houses on the reservation, our home was lighted with kerosene lamps. Our heat came from two wood-burning stoves—one huge barrel stove that was used only for heating and another stove that was used for both cooking and heating. We also used these stoves to heat water for our baths, which we took in a large, round tub.

As a boy, one of my chores was to keep enough wood piled outside the door to burn through the cold winter nights. I remember chopping both green wood and dry wood. This combination made a fire that lasted all night. I spent many winter evenings near the warm fire sketching by the light of a kerosene lamp.

From my earliest childhood, I loved to draw and sketch. My mother was often bothered by the constant disappearance of our family's writing tablet. My desire to sketch my surroundings continued

Drying Corn, 1971

Red Lake residents gathered in town for events *(above)*, but most of them lived and worked in the woodlands *(below)* outside the reservation's towns.

even during a temporary blindness that I experienced as a child. When I was five years old, I contracted a disease called trachoma. This ailment was common among Indian families in those days, and it often caused total blindness. I was lucky and recovered my sight completely.

WINTER WORK AND FUN

While I was growing up, each season of the year meant the beginning of a new round of activities for the people at Red Lake. Winter was the time of year for hunting and trapping. One of my duties was to snare rabbits for our food supply, and I remember having my own trap line when I was very young. Every day I walked from trap to trap with my companion, a big dog that looked like a collie.

From the traps I collected the day's catch, which usually amounted to three or four rabbits. The rabbits that I snared were hung in a little shed near our house. This shed was our frozen food locker, where we kept our wild game until my mother needed it for a meal.

The shed stored venison (deer meat), bear, moose, ducks, geese, quail, squirrels, raccoons, and fish, as well as rabbits. Rabbit was one of my favorite foods. My mother made a delicious stew by adding vegetables, wild rice, and seasoning to the delicately flavored rabbit. It was a special treat to eat the reheated stew before going to bed.

One of our staple foods during the winter was venison. My father and brothers had little trouble finding deer tracks in the deep winter snow, and they shot many deer. But it hurt me to see a deer slaughtered. I often watched these graceful animals in the woods during the day, and in the evenings I would sketch them. I never shot a deer, and as I grew older, my desire not to harm any animal became even stronger. Other than rabbits, the only animal I ever hunted as a little boy was the squirrel.

In addition to hunting rabbits, deer, and other wild game, the Red Lake Chippewa also did some winter fishing—a difficult task when the lakes were entirely frozen over. To fish, the men chopped holes in the thick ice and then lowered a line with a bright lure and a hook on

Buildings such as this one were used to store food and equipment.

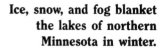

Ice, snow, and fog blanket the lakes of northern Minnesota in winter.

the end into the water. When a fish bit the hook, it was pulled up through the hole. Since the fish were frozen immediately after being caught, we had the finest in fresh-frozen fish.

Our winter activities were not always limited to work. One of the things I looked forward to in winter was a ride in our family sleigh. Our sleigh was very unusual because it was enclosed—it looked like a big rectangular box fastened to metal runners. My father's two strong horses pulled the sleigh through

the snow. Inside were benches, a table, and a stove to keep the passengers warm.

The driver sat outside in front of the enclosed sleigh. When my father got cold, another driver would take his place while he warmed himself inside. My mother would pack a lunch so that we could stay out all day and enjoy our ride, which was always a special treat for me. I have vivid memories of looking out the windows at the beautiful trees and clean snow as we glided along through the forests.

Frosty dewdrops cling to berries in early spring.

SPRING THAW

In the early spring, as the snow began to melt at Red Lake, we looked forward to one of nature's very special harvests. The sap started to flow in the maple trees, and we began to think about sweet maple sugar and maple sugar cakes.

When signs of warmer weather appeared, Red Lake Chippewa families collected all their equipment for harvesting maple sap. Then they set up camps and built temporary birch bark shelters near the maple groves. The elders called these maple sugar camps *Iskigamizigeng*, which means the "Sugar Bush."

The camp was a cooperative activity for the families at Red Lake. Because woodcutting occupied all my father's time, our family did not join in the maple sugar camp. But many of our relatives did, and I was always welcome to watch and to sketch them as they worked. Sketching their activities fascinated me, and the people I drew often asked to keep my pictures. They called me *gwiwizens odayan ozhibii'iganaak*, or the "little boy with the pencil."

The first step in harvesting maple sap was to tap the maple trees. This was done with a carved wooden peg that had a little groove down the center and a sharp, pointed end. The men tapped these pegs gently into the maple trees at a slight downward angle. From every peg, they hung a birch bark basket or an old syrup can. The sap flowed along the grooved pegs and down into the containers.

Every morning a man with a horse-drawn sleigh carried large washtubs from tree to tree, gathering the sap from each container. After each can or basket had been emptied, it was hung back on the peg to catch the next day's flow of sap.

At the camps, the sap was poured into large, black iron kettles that hung over hot fires. The sap was cooked until most of the water boiled off, leaving a

Maple Sugar Spring, 1970

thick syrup. It took 30 to 40 gallons of the sweet, watery sap to make one gallon of maple syrup. Some of the syrup was poured into large troughs, where women stirred the liquid gently with flat wooden paddles. Soon the syrup was transformed into fine grains of golden sugar.

Some syrup was poured into small wooden molds, where it hardened into little maple cakes. After many hours of smelling the sweet aroma of cooking sap, we children could hardly wait to eat the sugar and the candy. For a special treat, we poured hot syrup on the snow and let it harden. Then we could pull it back and forth like taffy until we had a soft, chewy candy.

After about two weeks, the sap in the trees began to turn bitter, and the people gathered their things together and returned home with their harvest. Many families took sugar and syrup to Bemidji, the nearest large city, where they sold it to grocery stores and tourist shops.

Red Lake Fishermen, 1946/1961

Selling maple sugar, however, was not a major livelihood at Red Lake. More important was the commercial fishing industry. Red Lake Chippewa families caught huge quantities of fish in the spring, and many of these fish were sold and shipped to areas outside of Red Lake. The best fish in the lake were walleye pike, and the Red Lake fisheries got large contracts for catching them.

When the ice began to break up and melt in the big lakes, fishing crews would prepare their fishing nets. In the evenings, the men rowed their boats to the fishing grounds, often three or four miles out in the lake. There they set their nets in the deep water.

The next morning, at about 5:00 A.M., men, women, and children would gather at the docks. As a little boy, I always looked forward to the excitement of these early morning gatherings. The men would board their hand-built boats, two men to a boat. They would row out to the fishing grounds and pull up the nets filled with pike.

Very few other kinds of fish were caught in the nets, because the Red Lake fishermen understood fish habits. Knowing the territories and water depths preferred by the different types of fish, the fishing crews put their nets in just the right places to catch walleye pike. At times the crews had such a good catch that they had to make two trips.

When the boats came in, we immediately began to take the fish out of the nets and put them in boxes of crushed ice. Then trucks from the fisheries came to pick up the boxes. We often took home some of the fresh fish and cooked them.

Not all of the fish at Red Lake were caught by professional fishermen. As a boy, I loved to go fishing with my friends. We often packed a lunch and spent the whole day fishing in small rivers and streams. Our simple fishing poles were made of willow sticks, and we used minnows and worms to bait our hooks. We

fished for bass, crappies, perch, pike, and many other fish that lived in the streams. Our fishing season began in the springtime and lasted all through the summer.

SUMMER GAMES

The summer season was a time to get together with other children for outdoor activities and games. Hide-and-seek, kick-the-can, and other games were the same ones played by girls and boys everywhere. Sometimes we built forts or platform tree houses in the woods, constructing them out of branches and logs.

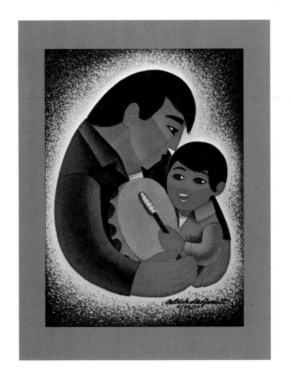

Father and Child, 1970

Most of the toys we played with were made by our parents or grandparents. Mothers made little leather dolls with beadwork trimmings for the girls. Fathers made miniature wooden cradle boards for the girls and carved wooden

Basket Maker, 1970

Women perform a dance at the Red Lake Pow-Wow.

toys for the boys. Some of the little wooden guns they made were very detailed.

In the imaginative games we played, we created a world all our own. We especially liked to play circus, complete with clowns, trained animals, and Kool-Aid or lemonade, which we sold to the adults. Our pet dogs, cats, and tamed raccoons and chipmunks often became our trained circus animals.

The summer event that everyone, both adults and children, looked forward to most was the Red Lake Pow-Wow. The traditional **pow-wows** of our ancestors had been meetings of Chippewa leaders for the purpose of solving problems. But when I was a boy, the pow-wow was mainly a social activity.

Lasting for four days in July, the pow-wow was the most colorful and exciting event of the year. Families came from other reservations in Minnesota and even from other states to participate. White tourists were invited, too, and they enjoyed the activities almost as much as we did.

The Red Lake Pow-Wow could be compared to a fair. Display booths, where people sold food and handmade crafts, were set up in a large circle. During the winter, the women had worked on quilts, beadwork, and goods made of leather and birch bark. These beautiful items were sold at the pow-wow, along with homemade bread, maple sugar, and wild rice.

Dancing was one of the most colorful events at the pow-wow. I was always fascinated by the skill and grace of the dancers who competed for prizes.

My people took great pride in expressing themselves through the art of dancing, and I loved to watch their twisting, turning movements as they kept time to the beat of the drums.

The costumes that the dancers wore were beautifully handcrafted. They were usually made of black velvet or felt. Intricate floral beadwork designs in bright colors like red, yellow, and turquoise were sewn on the black background. Making these designs required hours of careful work, and the finished costumes were among the most beautiful expressions of Chippewa art.

Another pow-wow event that I enjoyed was the moccasin game, which was played by two teams of four players each. Each member of one team stood in front of a moccasin, under which a marble was hidden. Three of the moccasins concealed ordinary marbles, but one moccasin hid a special "steelie" marble.

A player from the other team tried to guess which moccasin hid the special marble. The players on the first team had to keep a straight face—a gesture or facial expression might give away the team's secret. This game was very popular when I was young, and people often played it in their homes during the long winter months.

The greased pole contest was another challenge to everyone at the pow-wow. A tall pole was covered with heavy grease. Anyone could try to climb it,

and whoever succeeded was given an award. It was always fun to watch the climbers' attempts, even though most were unsuccessful.

The pow-wow was a time when old friends were reunited and new friends were made. Even as an adult, I continued to enjoy taking my family back to Red Lake, where we visited family and friends and attended various celebrations. And the biggest event for us was always the Red Lake Pow-Wow.

FALL HARVEST

As summer ended, my people began to prepare for the wild rice harvest, which was the most important event of the fall season. Wild rice, or *mahnomin*, was one of our staple foods, and it was prepared in a variety of ways. It could be cooked and used as a cereal or combined with meat and vegetables in main dishes like the rabbit stew my mother made.

Wild rice was usually ready to harvest in early September. Everyone in the family helped with the harvest—adult men and women gathered and processed the rice, and the children were responsible for chores such as collecting firewood.

Chippewa Dancer, 1964

Red Lake was one of the few areas in the region where wild rice was not plentiful. So Red Lake families traveled to the White Earth Reservation, which was about 50 miles away. The White Earth Chippewa were happy to share their rice with the people from Red Lake.

Wild rice is a grain that grows on long stalks, like wheat or barley. But unlike other grains, wild rice grows best in shallow, clay-bottomed lakes. Rice fields have always looked to me like wheat fields sitting in the middle of a lake.

Harvesting wild rice was a skill that took many years of experience to learn. Rice harvesters knew that the grains of wild rice do not ripen all at the same time. So they took only the rice that was ready and left the remaining kernels to ripen for a few days.

Hand-built boats with boxes in the middle were used for the harvest. A man standing in the front of the boat would move it through the field with a long pole. A ricing partner, usually a woman, sat in back and gathered the rice. She used two tapered flails, which were cedar sticks about 18 inches long. With one flail, she would bend the rice stalks over the boat. With another flail, she gently tapped the ripened rice so that it fell into the boxed area of the boat. When the boats were filled, the harvesters returned to shore, where the rice was stored in containers.

A man and a woman harvest wild rice.

Wild Rice Harvest (Harvesting the Wild Rice), 1969

After all the rice had been harvested, it was put in large metal kettles and hung over a fire for **parching.** In the parching process, the rice kernels were heated until their tough coverings, or hulls, burst open. Then the hulls and kernels were stirred gently.

After parching, the rice was poured into a hole in the ground that was lined with buckskin (soft leather). Pegs held the buckskin down on all sides. A person called the trampler, or *mamishkoogum,* then danced in the rice to separate the hulls from the kernels. The trampler, usually a man, had to wear spotlessly clean moccasins that had never touched the ground. According to a Chippewa legend, the rice harvest would be poor the following year if the trampler did not have clean moccasins.

When the trampler finished, he turned the rice over to the women. They put a portion of the rice into a large, flat birch basket. Then they picked the basket up and poured the rice into another similar basket. As the rice was poured, the wind blew away the hulls, leaving only the kernels.

After this process—called **winnowing**—was repeated 30 or 40 times, the rice was clean and ready for use or storage. Wild rice prepared in the traditional way left the long grains whole, whereas modern commercial methods often break the grains of rice.

After the two-week harvest was completed, the Red Lake families returned to their homes. Soon the rice fields and lakes would be frozen over, and the yearly cycle of activities would begin again.

Schools at Red Lake

During the 1920s, government-run or church-run **boarding schools** were the main educational institutions for Native Americans at Red Lake. A Christian church operated St. Mary's Mission Boarding School, the first school that DesJarlait attended. The **Bureau** **of Indian Affairs** (BIA), a government agency set up to supervise Native American reservations, ran the government schools.

BIA officials forced parents to send their children to boarding schools, often by threatening to withhold much-needed food vouchers from those who refused to cooperate. By keeping the children away from their homes,

Family bonds were very strong in the Chippewa culture, and older family members often took on the responsibility of educating the children. This practice changed when boarding schools opened on reservations.

Red Lake's boarding schools included St. Mary's Mission Boarding School *(top)* and Red Lake Boarding School *(bottom)*.

administrators and teachers found it easier to suppress the students' Native American customs and to introduce in their place the language, dress, and religion of the white people. Officials claimed that the students' success depended on their ability to adopt the lifeways of the mainstream culture of the United States.

After people began to protest the goals and functions of the boarding schools, regular day schools gradually replaced the live-in schools. In 1923 the first public school opened on the Red Lake reservation. By 1935 construction had begun on Red Lake Senior High School—the public school from which Patrick DesJarlait was graduated in 1939.

2
EXPERIENCING A WIDER WORLD

My first school was St. Mary's Mission Boarding School in the town of Redby. All the Chippewa schoolchildren had to live at the school, even though some of our homes were only half a mile away. On some weekends, we had home visitation privileges. But during the week, we lived in dormitories and ate all our meals at St. Mary's.

Many families needed the school's help to feed their children, since jobs were hard to find and some people were very poor. At school, the children could eat fruit, eggs, and milk—foods that they seldom had at home. St. Mary's also provided uniforms for the children to wear.

Our lives at St. Mary's were dominated by Catholic traditions. In the mornings, we went to Mass before breakfast. My teachers were nuns and priests, and they taught us about the church, as well as about the usual academic subjects.

I remember that strict regulations regarding customs and language were placed on us. We were not allowed to speak to one another in Chippewa or to participate in activities related to our heritage. Traditional Chippewa games, dancing, and crafts were forbidden. By imposing these restrictions, the school hoped to encourage us to accept the white people's way of life.

Chippewa Dancer, **1970**

Mother and Child, 1970

was always a small tree in our living room with presents from our parents under the boughs. We enjoyed our vacation, and we never looked forward to going back to the school routine.

When I was about seven years old, my mother died. This was a period of sadness and change in our family. The older children assumed many of the chores and responsibilities of the household. In time my father remarried, and we moved to a nice house in the town of Red Lake.

At about the time of our move, I was transferred from St. Mary's to the Red Lake Boarding School. My friends and I looked forward to this change, because we knew we would have more freedom and more time for sports and activities. At St. Mary's, our religious obligations had left us little time for play.

But, in some ways, life at the Red Lake school was similar to life in the mission school. We slept in dormitories and ate all our meals at school. Every Sunday we marched a mile and a half to the mission for church services, even though temperatures in the winter would sometimes fall to −25° F or colder. And we were forbidden to use Chippewa customs and language. During the summers

While we were at the school, we missed our families and our homes. Sometimes my mother would let me know when she was coming to the village during the week, and I would plan to sneak out and meet her on the road. She always brought me a sweet treat or a piece of fruit.

We all looked forward to the church holidays that were celebrated at St. Mary's. Christmas was especially exciting, and everyone in the community joined in the celebration at the mission school. We usually spent a few days at home during the holidays, too. There at home, however, we were not under these restrictions, and we returned to the ways of our people.

But we did have more time for going to movies and for enjoying other kinds of recreation. I also continued my artwork. At St. Mary's, some of the nuns had encouraged my drawing and had given me religious subjects to sketch. But I remember having my ears pulled by the priests because I was sketching during study time.

At Red Lake Boarding School, I was allowed to plan decorations for school affairs. In the school's workshop, I became interested in carving and in building things out of wood. My father was a skilled carpenter and appreciated my interest in woodwork.

Although my teachers at Red Lake Boarding School allowed me to sketch during study time, I don't remember getting much encouragement from them. In those days, art was not considered a practical career for a reservation Indian. I thought that I would always live at Red Lake and that I would eventually earn my living in the lumber mill or at the fisheries. It didn't occur to me that there was any other way of life open to me. This changed, however, when I transferred to the Pipestone Boarding School in Pipestone, a small town in the southwestern corner of Minnesota.

Children at reservation boarding schools had to clean and do other chores after school.

A TURNING POINT

My experience at Pipestone Boarding School was an important turning point for me. During those years, I realized for the first time that there was something more than reservation life.

At Pipestone we had new opportunities to meet white people and to learn about their way of life. We made extra money by doing yard work, painting, and other part-time jobs for white families in town. The families were always very friendly and sometimes invited us to have Sunday dinner with them. In addition to meeting white families, I got acquainted with my Indian classmates, who came from all over the United States. These experiences had an influence on my attitudes and my plans for the future.

There were many new activities and new things to explore at Pipestone. The world-famous Pipestone Quarry was located close to our school. This quarry is the only deposit of **pipestone** in the world, as far as anyone knows. For centuries, Indian people have used pipestone to carve ceremonial pipes. Groups from all over North America have traveled to this quarry just to get pipestone.

Before pipestone is exposed to air, the red mineral is fairly soft and easy to

Indian workers at Pipestone Quarry mine the soft, carveable rock.

Pipestone could be cut and carved with simple saws and knives.

carve. I liked to carve souvenir items out of pipestone, and I earned extra money by selling my carvings to tourist shops.

One of my most important activities during these years was my work with the Boy Scouts. I was an active member of a Boy Scout troop for three years, and I earned badges in woodcarving and art. My most outstanding memory was a Boy Scout trip to Sioux Falls, South Dakota. For this outing, I created a display of artwork for our troop. The display included several paintings of the lifeways of my people and a model of a canoe.

Although the teachers at school did not encourage us to use our native languages and customs, they did accept my drawings and paintings of Chippewa life. They encouraged my artistic abilities and took a greater interest in me than my previous teachers had taken. I was pleased also because the teachers at Pipestone were constantly giving me art projects to do. All these things added to my enjoyment of school and gave me a feeling of acceptance and confidence that had an important influence on my future career.

By the time I entered Red Lake Senior High, my experiences at Pipestone had given me the confidence to get involved in many extracurricular activities. I had always been very interested in music, as well as in art. I was a member of the school choir and band at Pipestone, and I continued these activities in high school. The instruments I liked most were the tenor saxophone and the clarinet.

At Red Lake High, four fellow students and I formed a small dance band with three saxophones, a trumpet, and a drum. We had mostly summer bookings, and we played for the tourists in the areas surrounding Red Lake. We were never sure whether we were popular because of our talent or because we were an "Indian combo"—a novelty in those days. But whatever the reason, we enjoyed the experience and the chance to meet people from all over the country.

Summer was a time for work, too. During high school, I had a summer job with the Civilian Conservation Corps (CCC). This was an agency authorized by the federal government to hire unemployed young men for jobs in conservation.

At Red Lake, CCC workers lived in a camp on the reservation. Our job was to maintain and improve the forest environment. We cleaned along the roadways, pulled gooseberry bushes, which were harmful to tree growth, and dug firebreaks. This was hard manual labor, but I liked it until I developed a severe allergy to poison ivy. In the summers that followed, I did building maintenance jobs for the Red Lake Tribal Council, which is the government of the Red Lake Chippewa.

CHOOSING TO BECOME AN ARTIST

The experiences and opportunities I had during my three years at Red Lake Senior High School strongly influenced my choice of a future career. For the first time in my student life, I felt free to express myself through art.

There were not many students who were involved in artistic activities, because art courses were not offered then. Most of my artistic work involved making decorations and scenery for school proms and plays. Although it was usually a lot of hard work, I liked creating scenery for the plays. This experience had a lot to do with my later interest in mural art.

One of my high school teachers remains very dear in my memories because of her encouragement and her deep personal interest in my artistic abilities. This kind and compassionate lady was Miss Ross, my English teacher, and she played an important role in my decision about my future. Miss Ross directed all the school plays, and I worked under her supervision in creating the sets. Many times, if I had finished my assignments, she let me cut her classes to sketch or work on art projects.

Miss Ross's attitude was different from that of the other teachers, many of whom could not imagine an Indian student in any environment other than the reservation. She often said to me, "Someday I want to hear great things about you." These words motivated my growing curiosity about art and about career opportunities in other parts of the country.

Miss Ross encouraged me to explore the field of art, and she kept me supplied with art materials, art publications, and books that she bought with her own money. Sometimes she'd visit Saint Paul—the capital of Minnesota—on weekends or during vacations. Before leaving, she would ask me what materials I needed. I looked forward to her return, so I could see what she had picked out for my work and study.

Miss Ross was interested in Chippewa culture, so I felt free to continue sketching my people and their customs. After my exposure to the white people's way of life, I found that I had a renewed interest in Red Lake traditions. Many of the Chippewa customs were becoming more and more meaningful to me, and I continued to observe them and to record them on paper. I also began to research and sketch the colors and the symbolism of Chippewa beadwork designs.

Chippewa Preparing for Battle, **1971**

Saint Paul Public Library

After Christmas vacation in my senior year, I had to decide what career to pursue. My artwork was becoming more professional, and I could begin to imagine a career in the field of **commercial art**. I asked Miss Ross to bring books from Saint Paul's libraries that would tell me more about commercial art. As the final weeks of high school passed, I became more certain that art would be a practical way for me to earn a living.

My decision became final when I received a year's scholarship to study art at Arizona State College in Phoenix. This award was presented to me at graduation by the Bureau of Indian Affairs. During the following summer, I continued to work for the tribal council, doing house painting and maintenance, and saved my money for clothes and the trip to Phoenix.

NEW PLACES AND NEW STYLES
Soon after arriving in Phoenix, I enrolled in art appreciation classes at Arizona

State College. These courses introduced me to the work of the great artists of the world, and I began learning to analyze the styles and designs of various artists. Such courses are common now, but then they were completely new and fascinating to me.

I also found that other Indian students from the Southwest were painting in a completely different style than I was. My style was almost photographically realistic, whereas they presented their subject matter in a flat, profile style that reminded me of ancient Egyptian art.

I lived at the Phoenix Boarding School, which was just a few blocks from the Phoenix Indian School. In the afternoons, I took various classes at the Indian school. This is where I learned about mural painting and fresco, which is a process of painting on wet plaster walls with water-based paint. My Southwestern friends and I worked as a team, combining our different styles to create an interesting end product. This was a great experience in communication for all of us.

I also took classes in pottery and in the preparation of art materials, and these classes added to my knowledge of art. But the more I learned about other forms of art, the more I saw that sketching and painting were the best ways for me to use my talents.

Art students at Arizona State College took classes in the Fine Arts Annex.

DesJarlait's Work During World War II

In 1941 Japan bombed Pearl Harbor, a U.S. military base in the Hawaiian Islands in the Pacific Ocean. This event marked the entry of the United States into World War II (1939–1945). Japanese Americans, who lived mainly on the Pacific coast of the United States, became the targets of some U.S. political leaders. These officials claimed that people of Japanese descent might spy or even enlist in the Japanese forces to help Japan win the war.

The U.S. Congress passed a new law in 1942 that required all people of Japanese ancestry—even those who were U.S. citizens—to move to **relocation camps**. Set up mainly in desert areas, the relocation centers were unpleasant places where Japanese Americans were forced to live for several years.

During World War II, a Japanese American girl waited with her family's luggage before leaving for a relocation camp in 1942.

WESTERN DEFENSE COMMAND AND FOURTH ARMY
WARTIME CIVIL CONTROL ADMINISTRATION
Presidio of San Francisco, California
April 1, 1942

INSTRUCTIONS
TO ALL PERSONS OF
JAPANESE
ANCESTRY

Living in the Following Area:

All that portion of the City and County of San Francisco, State of California, lying generally west of the northsouth line established by Junipero Serra Boulevard, Worchester Avenue, and Nineteenth Avenue, and lying generally north of the east-west line established by California Street, to the intersection of Market Street, and thence on Market Street to San Francisco Bay.

All Japanese persons, both alien and non-alien, will be evacuated from the above designated area by 12:00 o'clock noon Tuesday, April 7, 1942.

No Japanese person will be permitted to enter or leave the above described area after 8:00 a. m., Thursday, April 2, 1942, without obtaining special permission from the Provost Marshal at the Civil Control Station located at:

1701 Van Ness Avenue
San Francisco, California

The Civil Control Station is equipped to assist the Japanese population affected by this evacuation in the following ways:

1. Give advice and instructions on the evacuation.
2. Provide services with respect to the management, leasing, sale, storage or other disposition of most kinds of property including: real estate, business and professional equipment, buildings, household goods, boats, automobiles, livestock, etc.
3. Provide temporary residence elsewhere for all Japanese in family groups.
4. Transport persons and a limited amount of clothing and equipment to their new residence, as specified below.

The Following Instructions Must Be Observed:

1. A responsible member of each family, preferably the head of the family, or the person in whose name most of the property is held, and each individual living alone, will report to the Civil Control Station to receive further instructions. This must be done between 8:00 a. m. and 5:00 p. m., Thursday, April 2, 1942, or between 8:00 a. m. and 5:00 p. m., Friday, April 3, 1942.

Signs *(inset)* **informed people of Japanese descent about the U.S. government's plan to move them away from their homes and businesses. At the relocation camp in Poston, Arizona** *(above)*, **residents lived in dreary, crowded quarters.**

For about six months in 1942, DesJarlait worked as the art director at a relocation camp at Poston, Arizona. After receiving orders to join the U.S. Navy, he reported to San Diego, California, where he spent the next three and a half years. During this time, DesJarlait worked with animation artists making instructional films for the navy.

3

PRINTING PRESSES, ART SHOWS, AND HOW-TO FILMS

Toward the spring of 1942, when the school term at Phoenix was ending, I realized that I would have to go into military service. This was during World War II, and the Japanese air force had attacked the U.S. naval base at Pearl Harbor earlier that winter. All young men in the United States had to contribute to the war effort.

WORKING WITH THE JAPANESE

One day, a teacher from the Indian school called me to his office. A tall white man dressed in a buckskin jacket, boots, and a Western hat greeted me. He introduced himself as a representative of the Bureau of Indian Affairs and the U.S. Army. He wanted to inter-view me because of the recommendations of my teachers. The representative offered me a job as an art supervisor in a Japanese relocation camp at Poston, Arizona.

Someone was needed at the Arizona camp to organize an art department and to supervise the printing of a camp newspaper. I accepted the position and moved to Poston after the school term ended. Poston was in the middle of the desert, and the hot, dry climate there was unbelievable, especially for a person from Red Lake, Minnesota. Temperatures climbed above 100° F every day, and it seemed that the wind seldom ceased. The wind blew so much dust into my room that maids had to sweep it three times a day to keep it clean.

Some of the Japanese people at the camp were very talented and had strong art backgrounds. Many of them had worked in Hollywood movie studios before their relocation. These people appreciated having art projects to keep them occupied in their strange new environment. I had great sympathy for the Japanese, because they had been placed in a situation similar to that of my own people. They were forced to move from their homes to remote and restricted areas, as many Native Americans had been forced to do.

Apparently our art department at the camp was successful. In addition to working with the printing press, we got approval to experiment with various kinds of art. My superiors also gave me permission to take our group of artists into the mountains on Sundays to sketch and paint. We had art shows, too, and these shows displayed an array of talent in painting, ceramics, watercolor, lithograph, and sculpture. Government employees donated money for the prizes at these shows.

A small post office allowed people to communicate with friends and family members outside the relocation camp.

A STINT IN THE NAVY

Five months after the camp's art department was organized, I received orders for induction into the navy. I reported to San Diego, California, where I was issued a uniform and was scheduled for seamanship training. But after a month on this duty, I was transferred to the Visual Aids Department at the base.

This department produced instructional films and brochures for the navy. The films were used to demonstrate the assembly of torpedos and other jobs.

Many of these films were animated, created by 14 talented animation artists from the Walt Disney and MGM studios. Working with these artists, I learned many skills that prepared me for the future I hoped to have in commercial art.

For the next three and a half years, I worked in the Visual Aids Department and got to know my fellow artists. On weekends we were free to leave the base, and several of the artists rented old garages in the area and fixed them up to use as studios. After the garages were cleaned and painted, they became pleas-

The naval base at San Diego was a busy place during the war.

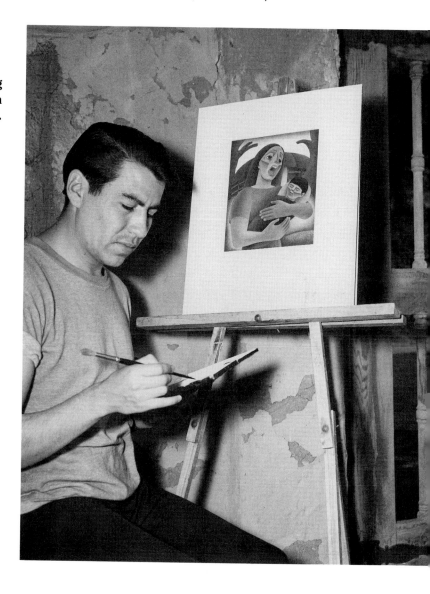

DesJarlait was developing his painting style while in San Diego.

ant places in which to work. During this time, the subjects for my weekend painting came from my memories of Red Lake.

Friends who saw my work told their friends about the unusual colors and images, and eventually I was asked to have a solo exhibition at the Fine Arts Gallery in San Diego. Every painting was sold by the end of the show.

In 1945, shortly after this show, I was discharged from the navy. Without hesitation I was homeward bound.

Growth of an Artist

Upon returning to Minnesota, DesJarlait married Ramona Needham, a member of the Red Lake Chippewa Band whom he had known since his schooldays at Red Lake. In 1946 they had a son, Robert, who would be the first of their five children.

Patrick and Ramona DesJarlait

DesJarlait spent a year painting at the reservation, working to perfect his style. The family then moved to the Saint Paul area, where he found employment in commercial art. At the same time, he continued to work on his paintings, which were winning awards at artists' exhibitions throughout the United States.

After establishing himself as a successful artist, DesJarlait devoted time to speaking in schools about his art and his heritage. At these presentations, he hoped to teach young people about the importance of Chippewa tradition and culture.

A Native American ricer glides through the long stalks of wild rice on a quiet lake.

4

HOME AGAIN

It was good to be back at Red Lake. I knew that I would eventually have to look for a job in commercial art, but first it was important for me to take the time to develop a painting style of my own. I spent the next year experimenting with pencil and tracing paper and doing sketch after sketch. Finally I arrived at a style that satisfied me. The painting *Red Lake Fishermen* was the first example of the brush technique and style that became my trademark.

Red Lake Fishermen and all my following paintings were done with watercolors. Bright colors have always been interesting to me, and I used very little water to dilute my pigments. Mixed this way, my paint was thick and kept its vibrant color.

Maple Sugar Time, 1946

Northern Minnesota's forests and lakes became the setting of many of DesJarlait's paintings.

Details from
Red Lake Fishermen, 1946/1961
(entire painting shown on
page 16)

Before beginning *Red Lake Fishermen,* I spent many hours observing and sketching the fishermen at work in their boats. Next I sketched my painting on the final piece of composition paper and painted in the background areas with a large brush. With a very small brush, I then began to fill in these areas with a series of tiny brush strokes. The small strokes were applied to create a rounded, moving effect and to keep the viewer's eye focused on the points of interest in the painting.

These individual little strokes were to me like the tiny particles that make up our world and everything in it. I worked hard to perfect my technique, and I prob-

ably took three times as long as most artists do to complete a painting.

The year I spent at Red Lake was a time for keen observation. I wanted to record everything I could learn about my people and their way of life. I had strong personal feelings about keeping my subject matter unique and original, and I also felt compelled to tell the story of my people through my paintings. I have always wanted to show others the interest and pride that the Chippewa take in their families, their ceremonies, and their environment.

After a year at Red Lake, it was time for me to look for a way to earn a living with my artistic skills. I knew I would someday be able to use the storehouse of information I had gathered for my painting. But I thought that the immediate solution to my need for financial support would probably come from a job in commercial art, in which I could use the skills and training I had gained in the navy.

I began looking for a job in the Twin Cities area of Minneapolis and Saint Paul, approximately 300 miles south of Red Lake. The knowledge and abilities I had acquired through the years eventually got me a job at Reid Ray Films, Inc., in Saint Paul.

During the years that followed, I worked as both a freelance and full-time commercial artist. I took jobs at various film companies and advertising agencies and spent a number of years with the visual aids department of Northern Ordnance, a division of a large company that manufactures defense systems for the U.S. Navy.

Grinding Corn, **date unknown**

One of the highlights of my commercial art career was an assignment from Campbell-Mithun, Inc., one of the largest advertising companies in the Midwest. Along with some other artists, I was chosen to create a new television advertising campaign for the Theodore Hamms Brewery. We worked for many days over our drawing boards, only to come up with several ideas that were rejected.

The company wanted to project an image of "the great outdoors." Their theme was "Land of Sky Blue Waters," and it seemed that an animated drawing of some woodland animals might be the answer. One of the most mischievous and delightful animals of the forest is the bear. At Red Lake, we knew that bears were not harmful unless they were aggravated. We usually found them playfully involved in simple pranks, like tipping over garbage cans.

After I had sketched quite a few animations of the playful woodland bear, I presented the idea to my superiors. They liked my ideas, and so did the Hamms Brewery. The creation of the Hamms bear was one of my most delightful accomplishments in commercial art.

For 26 years, I enjoyed a varied career in commercial art. But during those years, I kept turning back to what I had always wanted to do—painting my people. I always set aside a few hours each evening after work for personal creation and expression. My lovely wife, Mona, and my five children gave me the courage and the motivation to go on with my painting. Finally, I began to concentrate all my time and energy on painting rather than on commercial art.

The city of Saint Paul, where DesJarlait worked for a number of years, lies on the banks of the Mississippi River.

Woman and Blueberries, 1971

I had the good fortune to win recognition and a number of awards throughout the country. Companies, galleries, and private collectors purchased many of my paintings of Chippewa life. Finally, my dreams of what I wished to accomplish had become a reality.

As time went on, my life came to revolve completely around painting and around lecturing at public schools, colleges, and other educational institutions. I always sensed the deep interest that students had in the culture of my people. Even small children listened intently to my lectures on Chippewa customs.

Each of my paintings tells a story about some aspect of Chippewa life. It has always been my hope that my paintings will help to remind my people of their own heritage and that they, in turn, will inform other people about the traditional Chippewa way of life.

EPILOGUE

"There are several things that impress us about Patrick Des-Jarlait's work. One is the quiet sense of dignity that pervades his pictures. The figures go about their tasks with an intense focus and dedication. To us they display physical strength and dexterity, coupled with a gentle caring and devotion for the objects they make or the foodstuffs they harvest. The artifacts portrayed reflect those that have been used for generations. The colors are intense and vibrant. The paintings nurture our love for the lakes and woodlands of the north."

Richard and Dorothy Nelson, owners of *Basket Maker* and *Drying Corn*, Duluth, MN.

"Patrick DesJarlait was one of the first respected 'modern' artists to have a following and to be an inspiration for many younger Native American artists after him. He also preserves a 'narrative' depiction of sugaring and other traditional activities that is valuable."

George Morrison, noted artist, member of the Grand Portage Chippewa Band, Grand Portage, MN.

"Patrick DesJarlait did not receive wide recognition or acclaim during his lifetime. Many years later, when scholars began to reexamine DesJarlait's work, many concluded that his paintings were pivotal in the development of Midwestern Native American art. Like a few other truly great Native American artists, DesJarlait developed a uniquely personal style. His love for his Ojibwe heritage and his care to record and preserve all of the details of Ojibwe ways of life, dance costumes, and craft objects are also characteristic of his art.

DesJarlait's paintings are now cherished by those who know them. They are in several museums throughout the country and in the hands of private collectors and friends of the artist. The Minnesota Museum of American Art's exhibition, 'Patrick DesJarlait and the Ojibwe Tradition,' included as many of these rare pieces as possible.

It is our hope that Patrick DesJarlait will continue to be remembered and honored through an appreciation of his paintings, which coincidentally bring us a heightened understanding of Ojibwe culture. More importantly, his art stirs our imagination and satisfies our search for beauty, with its vivid colors, animated forms, and exquisite detail."

Katherine Van Tassell, Acting Chief Curator, Minnesota Museum of American Art, Saint Paul, MN.

"In the late 1960s, Mary and I saw a painting done by Patrick DesJarlait. We were fascinated by the vivid colors and the strong figures as well as by the subject matter. We contacted him and were invited to his home. Patrick and his family were very warm and open people, and we developed a friendship.

Mary and I had been planning to start a maple syrup operation in northern Minnesota. We told Patrick that we would love to buy a painting that depicted the maple sugar season, if he ever completed a new work on that subject.

One day, several years later, we received an issue of the magazine *Conservation Volunteer* and saw on the cover a wonderful painting of maple sugaring, done by Patrick. We were even more surprised later that same day when Patrick called to say he had finished our painting and we should come to pick it up.

The painting now hangs in our home, and we have several other prints of Patrick's work in our lodge. We truly enjoy the wonderful art that Patrick has done and feel very lucky to have known such a warm and sensitive person."

Jim and Mary Richards, owners of *Maple Sugar Spring*, Callaway, MN.

"The importance of my father's art—from his perspective—was the manner in which he expressed his imagery. His paintings from 1946, *Red Lake Fishermen* and *Making Wild Rice*, stand as his most prolific pieces, through which he introduced a new way to visualize Native American people. The dynamic style that was expressed in these paintings wasn't derived from studying modernism and then developing a style based on modernistic concepts. Rather, he developed an art that was representational in content and that was expressed through a more natural modernism. And to my father, modernism was a natural expression of the Native American artist.

When he developed his style in 1946, my father simply drew and painted the human form in a way that other Native American artists had not. The style my father created represented his desire to break away from the traditional themes that had become a cliché in Southwestern Native American art. To him, the history that was depicted through Southwestern Native American art was important, but he felt there was also a need for other Native American fine artists to depict contemporary Native American existence of tribal cultures outside the Southwestern sphere of influence. His innovations in this area were his main accomplishments and contributions to Native American fine art.

When my father left us in November 1972, a paint brush was placed in his breast pocket. It was a tattered old brush, the hairs speckled and stained by the colors of many paints, the handle worn smooth and bare through many paintings. But it was one of his favorites, something familiar for him to take on his journey homeward to the Spirit World."

Robert DesJarlait, artist and owner of *Red Lake Fishermen* and *Chippewa Dancer* (1964), Minneapolis, MN.

boarding school A school where students live and attend classes during the school year. Native American children were sent to boarding schools where white educators tried to replace the children's traditional lifeways with U.S. mainstream culture, language, and dress.

Bureau of Indian Affairs A U.S. governmental agency that supervises Native American reservations and other tribal matters.

Chippewa A nation of Native American people living primarily in the states of Minnesota, Wisconsin, and Michigan, and the Canadian provinces of Manitoba and Ontario. The Chippewa are also known as the Anishinabe and as the Ojibway.

commercial art A combination of a variety of art forms used mainly in advertising and in other printed materials. Commercial artists paint, draw, photograph, and letter pieces of work to be used in books, films, logos, magazines, newsprint, packaging, and trademarks.

mission A religious center where people work to spread their beliefs among other groups. Missions near Native American communities often set up churches and schools.

parch To roast harvested wild rice to cook out the moisture and to loosen the hulls from the rice kernels.

pipestone A soft, carveable rock that is known to exist only near Pipestone, a town in southwestern Minnesota. Native Americans have used pipestone for centuries to make pipes and other carved objects.

pow-wow A Native American social gathering that includes dancing, games, and booths selling homemade foods and handmade arts and crafts.

relocation camp One of 10 centers set up in the western United States by the U.S. government during World War II. The government sent people of Japanese descent to live in the camps, which were poorly equipped, unsanitary, and crowded. Some U.S. officials felt Japanese people living in the United States might try to help Japan win the war.

reservation An area of land that a Native American group has kept through treaties, or agreements, with the U.S. government.

winnow To blow away the loosened hulls from rice kernels so only the edible rice is left.

PRONUNCIATION GUIDE

Anishinabe	ah-NISH-ehn-AH-bay
Bemidji	beh-MIJ-ee
Chippewa	CHIP-uh-wah
DesJarlait	deh-ZHAHR-lay
gwiwizens odayan	GWEE-wee-zahns oh-DY-ahn
ozhibii'iganaak	o-zhee-BEE-ee-gun-uk
Iskigamizigeng	is-kee-gum-ee-ZEE-ging
mahnomin	mah-NOH-mihn
mamishkoogum	mah-MISH-koo-gum
Ojibway	oh-JIHB-way
Ponemah	peh-NEE-mah

ACKNOWLEDGMENTS

Photo by Paul Howey, courtesy, Rod Wallace, Thunderbird Hotel, pp. 1, 27; © 1971, Star–Tribune/Minneapolis & Saint Paul, photo by Roy Swan, p. 5; Minnesota Historical Society, pp. 7, 24, 31, 49; Patrick Robert DesJarlait, Chippewa, "Mother/Child," 1972, watercolor, 30″ x 40″, Collection of The Heard Museum, photo courtesy, The Heard Museum, p. 9; courtesy, Dorothy and Richard Nelson Collection, pp. 10, 18; MN Hist. Soc., photos by Monroe Killy, pp. 11 (top), 12, 19; MN Hist. Soc., photos by Kenneth M. Wright, pp. 11 (bottom), 22, 43; Lucille Sukalo, p. 13; Lia E. Munson/Root Resources, p. 14; photo by John Borge, courtesy, Jim Richards, p. 15; Robert DesJarlait, pp. 16, 46; Charmaine DesJarlait, p. 20; courtesy, General Mills, Inc., p. 23; Beltrami County Historical Society, p. 25 (top); MN Hist. Soc., photo by A. A. Richardson, p. 25 (bottom); St. Benedict's Archives, St. Joseph, MN, p. 29; MN Hist. Soc., photo by C.E. Sogn, p. 30; Karen Sirvaitis/IPS, p. 34; courtesy, ASU Insight, p. 35; War Relocation Authority, National Archives, pp. 36, 37 (top); Arizona Historical Foundation, pp. 37 (bottom), 39; Minneapolis Public Library and Information Center, p. 40; San Diego Historical Society, Union–Tribune Collection, p. 41; The Philbrook Museum of Art, p. 45 (top); Kay Shaw, p. 45; CME–KHBB, p. 47; Paul Stafford/Minnesota Office of Tourism, p. 48.

Front cover: Minnesota Historical Society
Back cover (top): San Diego Historical Society, Union–Tribune Collection
Back cover (bottom): photo by Frank Agar, courtesy, Will Agar

INDEX

METRIC CONVERSION CHART		
WHEN YOU KNOW:	**MULTIPLY BY:**	**TO FIND:**
gallons	3.79	liters
inches	2.54	centimeters
miles	1.609	kilometers
degrees Fahrenheit	5/9 (after subtracting 32)	degrees Celsius